Clever RAINFOREST Questions

Annabelle Lynch

W FRANKLIN WATTS
LONDON • SYDNEY

First published in Great Britain in 2026 by Hodder & Stoughton
Copyright © Hodder & Stoughton Limited, 2026
All rights reserved.

Credits
Series Editor: Julia Bird
Series Designer: Peter Scoulding

Picture credits: Nature PL: Bence Mate 18-19; Theo Webb 36-37. iStock: Ksana-gribakina 10-11; Shutterstock: Arif_Vector 21b; Agnieszka Bacal 34; Birdtolk f cover bl, 12-13; Borneo Rimbawan 6-7; Mark Brandon f cover cr, 27b, 47b; T. Channels 28-29bg; Cobalt88 8-9; Aleksei Derin 19b; Designer Saidur 38-39c; Dirk Ercken f cover br; 40tr, 40br, 41t, 41cl, 46br; Max Filov 28b; Foxyliam 20b; Fullsuniverse 26l; Incomible 24; Eric Isselee 40tl, 41cr,41br; Rob Jansen 31t; Natee K Jinkadum 8-9 border; Komthing-Apec 28c; Lukas Kovarik f cover cl, 30; Li ji you 4-5; Lonvero 26-27bg; Leonardo Mercon 1,14br; Mr Black 20-21; Ms pics and more 27t; NikNajmuddin Photography 38-39; New Africa f cover cr, 2bl, 3tr, 16t, 16b, 17c; Nowaczyk 32-33; PaintDoor 13c; Travis Potter 35r; Valentina Razumova 21t; Reptiles4all 22-23; Andreas Ruiz 15; Sharp 31b; Valentina Shilkina 42-43; Joa Souza 32; Taweesak Sriwannawit 2br,16,17t; Alex Stemmer 40bl; Toltemara 29c; Tranle 29b; Vagonik 39tr; Kevin Wells Photography 26bl; Richard Whitcombe 44-45; White Shama 7c; WinWin artlab f cover tl, 25, 47t.

Every attempt has been made to clear copyright. Should there be any inadvertent omission please apply to the publisher for rectification.

HB ISBN: 978 1 4451 9233 8
PB ISBN: 978 1 4451 9234 5

Printed in Dubai

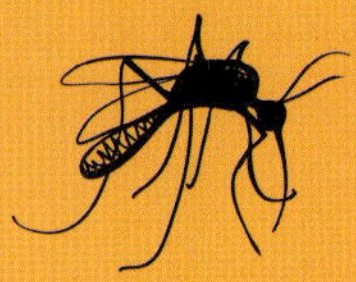

MIX
Paper | Supporting responsible forestry
FSC® C104740

Franklin Watts
An imprint of
Hachette Children's Group
Part of Hodder & Stoughton
Carmelite House
50 Victoria Embankment
London EC4Y 0DZ

An Hachette UK Company
www.hachette.co.uk
www.hachettechildrens.co.uk
The authorised representative in the EEA is Hachette Ireland, 8 Castlecourt Centre, Dublin 15, D15 XTP3, Ireland (email: info@hbgi.ie)

Contents

4	**Why is the rainforest so wet?**
6	**How many trees grow in the Amazon?**
8	**Why do plants love rainforest life?**
10	**How is the rainforest like a block of flats?**
12	**Which rainforest plant smells terrible?!**
14	**Where can you swim halfway up a tree?**
16	**Which rainforest plant eats flies?**
18	**Which rainforest reptile can walk on water?**
20	**How does the rainforest heal a toothache?**
22	**Can a spider really eat a bird?**
24	**Why do vines cuddle trees?**
26	**Which insects are all over the rainforest?**
28	**Can you get a coffee in the rainforest?**
30	**Which sleepy animal only poos once a week?**
32	**Can you live in the rainforest?**
34	**Which animal flies through the rainforest trees?**
36	**Where do apes sleep in nests?**
38	**Are there dry rainforests?**
40	**Just how poisonous is a poison dart frog?**
42	**How are rainforests like lungs?**
44	**Why are the rainforests disappearing?**
46	**Glossary**
47	**Find out more**
48	**Index**

Why is the rainforest ...

The clue is in the name – **IT RAINS A LOT THERE!**

There are two main types of rainforest, tropical and temperate. Tropical rainforest is found close to Earth's tropics. These lie either side of the equator, the imaginary band that stretches around the middle of Earth. Here, the weather is **HOT AND WET** all year round.

... so wet?

Temperate rainforest is much RARER. It is found further north or south in cooler places, close to the sea. These include the west coast of North and South America and parts of Great Britain, Japan, Australia and New Zealand. Temperate rainforests receive a lot of rain, which blows in from the nearby sea, and are humid and foggy.

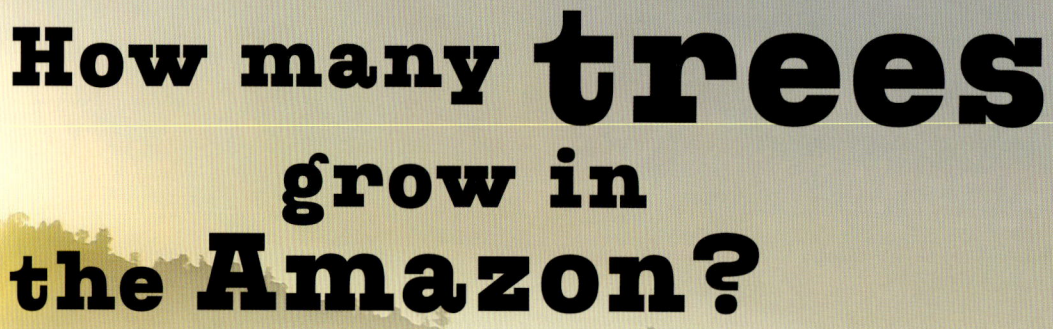

How many trees grow in the Amazon?

WE DON'T KNOW FOR DEFINITE, but it's estimated that there are an incredible 400 billion trees in the Amazon. That's 50 trees for every person on Earth!

The Amazon rainforest is the world's biggest rainforest by far. It stretches for an incredible 6.7 MILLION square kilometres, and spans nine different countries across South America. It's named for the mighty Amazon River, which flows through the rainforest.

The trees of the Amazon belong to an estimated 16,000 different species and include rubber trees, palms and the towering Brazil nut tree, for which the country of Brazil is named.

How many?
There are believed to be 3 trillion – or 3,000,000,000,000 – trees in the world!

Why do plants love rainforest life?

TWO WORDS – WARMTH AND SUNSHINE!

Plants LOVE sunny, damp conditions. They take in the energy in sunlight through their leaves, and water from the soil through their roots, and use it to make food. This is known as PHOTOSYNTHESIS.

The weather in tropical areas is especially sunny. Because Earth is slightly tilted in space, the Sun's rays strike the equator directly all year round, making it HOT. There is also lots of rain in areas close to the equator, so plants can take in plenty of water. And tropical weather stays about the same all year, so plants there don't have to go through cold winters.

All of these combine to make the tropical rainforest a PARADISE for plant life. Trees, shrubs, ferns, vines and colourful flowers all grow and thrive there!

How is a rainforest like a block of flats?

Because it is made up of different storeys or levels, just like a building!

The bottom level is the **FOREST FLOOR**. Here it is dark and shady, as the trees above block most of the sunlight, and few plants grow. Leaves, branches and fruit fall to the ground and rot away fast. Big animals, such as elephants, jaguars and giant anteaters, roam.

Above the forest floor is the **UNDERSTOREY**, where small plants and ferns thrive, and vines take root. Flying insects buzz around in the damp air and snakes coil around the mossy tree trunks.

Further up is the rainforest **CANOPY**, which is full of life! Monkeys, birds and sloths swing, fly and crawl high up in the treetops, feasting on nuts and fruits.

At the top of the rainforest is the **EMERGENT LAYER**, where the tallest trees rise up above the rest to reach the precious sunlight. Birds of prey, such as eagles, perch in the trees, along with some brave monkeys.

Which rainforest plant smells ...

THAT WOULD BE THE *RAFFLESIA*, otherwise known as the corpse (dead body) flower. Sounds nice, doesn't it?

... terrible?!

Rafflesia is found deep in the rainforest of Borneo, in south-east Asia. It is a parasite, meaning that it doesn't make its own food. Instead, it grows inside a vine, known as its host, and survives by taking in water and nutrients from the vine (RUDE!). Eventually, it emerges from its host as a huge flower, without roots, leaves or even a stem.

So why is the *Rafflesia* SO STINKY? Well, that's how it survives. The scent it gives out is like rotting meat, and it attracts flies, beetles and other insects. When they land on the flower, they get covered in wet, sticky pollen. They carry the pollen to another *Rafflesia* plant and pollinate it. The pollinated *Rafflesia* can now produce a new plant, and so the *Rafflesia* lives on.

Big stink!
The *Rafflesia* flower can grow to up to a metre across.

Where can you swim halfway up a tree?

Fancy having a swim while perched up high in the rainforest? Then you need to find a **BROMELIAD!**

Some of these amazing plants grow on rainforest trees, where they grip onto the tree's bark with their roots. Their colourful leaves are shaped and arranged so that rainwater runs down them to collect in a **POOL**, which the bromeliad takes in when it's needed.

These mini pools are teeming with life, and can form whole ecosystems! Tiny plant-like algae live here, fed by falling leaves, and are in turn food for small insects and their larvae, or young. In their turn, these insects and larvae are gobbled up by hungry **TADPOLES AND FROGS**, snails and even salamanders.

Watering hole
The tank bromeliad can store up to 20 litres of water.

Which rainforest plant ...

PITCHER PLANTS! These strange rainforest plants are NOT fussy eaters.

Pitcher plants grow in forests where the soil doesn't give them enough of the nutrients they need. So pitcher plants have a GENIUS way of topping up their diet – they gulp down insects, frogs and even rats!

They use sweet scents, bright colours and delicious nectar to lure their unlucky prey towards the rim of their tube-shaped leaves. The prey reaches hopefully for the nectar, but slips on the plant's wet rim and topples into the pitcher. Then – SNAP! The pitcher lid slams shut and the prey is trapped.

... eats flies?

The bottom of the pitcher is filled with liquid. The prey drowns in it, then its body is slowly broken down by juices in the liquid. The pitcher plant takes in the nutrients from the prey to feed itself and lives another day! SLURP.

YUK!
Some pitcher plants have even weirder tastes! One even munches on shrew poo – gross, but full of vital nutrients for the plant.

Which rainforest reptile can walk on water?

THE JESUS LIZARD.
This agile reptile doesn't just walk on water – it runs!

Jesus lizards are found in rainforests of Central America. They have lots of natural predators lurking in the rainforest, from bigger reptiles to birds. So Jesus lizards have a **CLEVER TRICK** to escape them – they run across water to safety!

They are able to do this because their back feet have an unusual adaptation: some of their toes have fringes of skin. On land these fringes are tucked in, but when the lizard hits the water they expand sideways, giving the lizard's feet a bigger SURFACE AREA. As they run, each step pushes down on the water, creating little pockets of air, which, together with the lizard's wide feet and speedy pace, keeps the lizard on top of, rather than below, the water.

Super sprinter
Jesus lizards can run between 10 and 20 metres over water. They are also good swimmers!

How does the rainforest heal a toothache?

Not just toothache, but infectious diseases and even some types of cancer. The rainforest is known as the world's MEDICINE CABINET as around a quarter of all medical drugs are based on rainforest plants.

Some amazing rainforest-based medicines include:

QUININE
This wonder drug is found in the bark of the Cinchona tree. It has been used for hundreds of years to treat the deadly illness malaria, which is spread by mosquitoes. Quinine has saved MILLIONS of lives.

COCA
Drugs taken from the leaves of the coca plant have been used as a **PAINKILLER** at the dentist, and for some vaccinations.

VINCRISTINE AND VINBLASTINE
These medicines come from the Madagascan **PERIWINKLE PLANT** and were originally used to treat the condition diabetes. They are now also used to treat the blood cancer, leukaemia, in children.

And there may be many more rainforest medicines yet to be discovered ...

Can a spider really eat ...

IT MIGHT NOT SEEM POSSIBLE, but there is indeed a species of rainforest spider that can eat birds!

The Goliath birdeater tarantula is found in the rainforests of South America, where it lives close to the ground in burrows and under rocks and roots. It doesn't weave a web to capture its prey. Instead, it comes out at night to hunt among the leaf litter. It first injects its victim with **POWERFUL VENOM.** Then it injects it again with digestive juices and eats by sucking it up. ICK!

... a bird?

The Goliath birdeater is named for its appetite for birds, but it doesn't actually eat them that often. It prefers to SNACK on other small rainforest animals, including insects, frogs, lizards and rats.

Giant spider!
The Goliath birdeater is the biggest spider around, with a body measuring up to 12 centimetres (cm) and legs adding another 28 cm or so. It's named after a GIANT from the Bible, Goliath.

Why do vines cuddle trees?

LIANA VINES are some of the rainforest's most common sights. These thick, woody creepers are a companion to many rainforest trees.

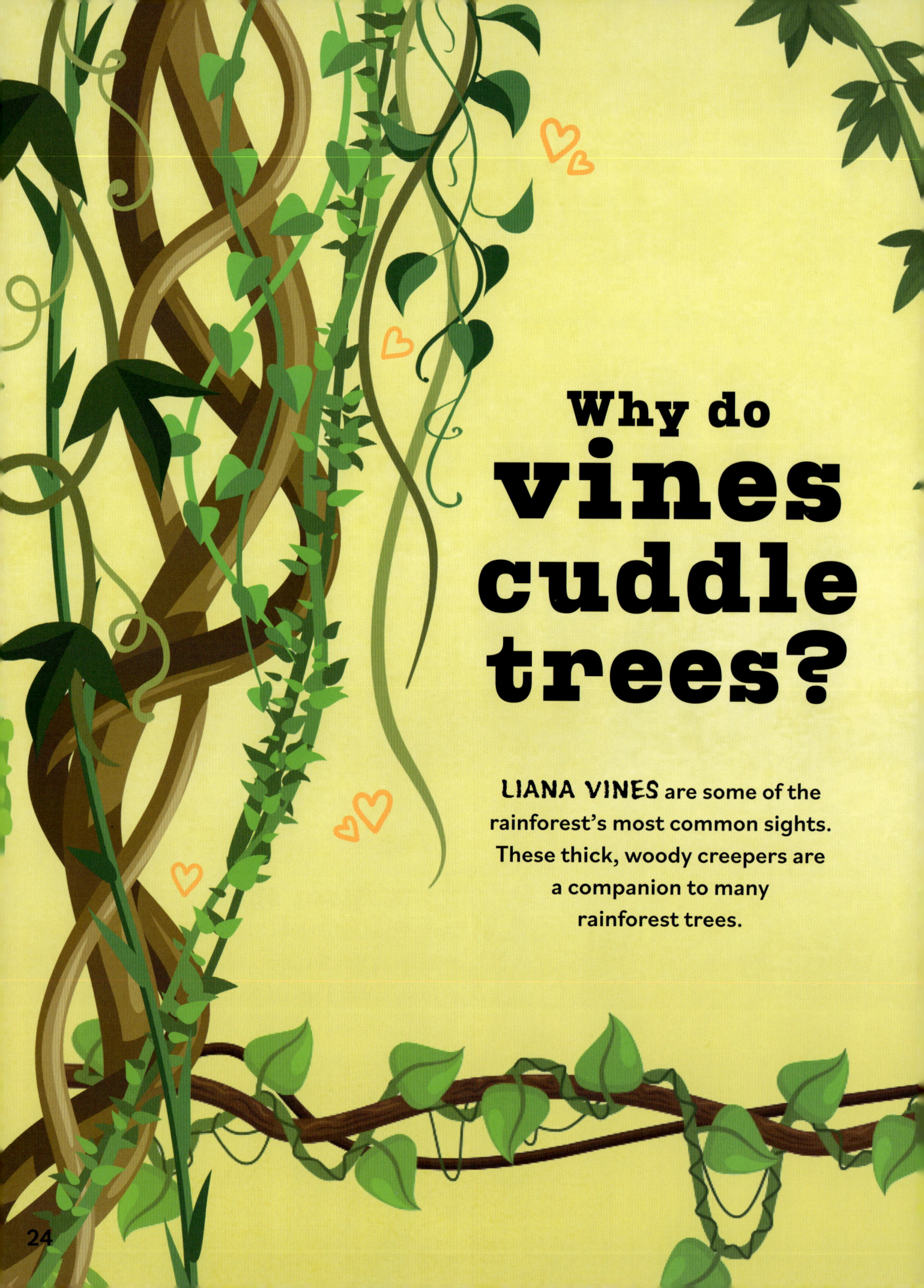

So why do lianas CURVE AND CURL around trees to grow? Well, like most rainforest plants, they need to reach the light! Their roots are planted in the rainforest soil, but lianas don't develop stems strong enough to help the vine to grow up from the floor. So lianas get a helping hand from a nearby tree!

Some lianas attach themselves to the tree by winding themselves around it. Others use thorns or even a type of glue to stick themselves to their companion. And now they can grow as tall as the tree, and reach the sunny canopy of the rainforest. AAH!

Which insects are all over the ...

ANTS! These small but sturdy insects are found EVERYWHERE in the rainforest, from the dark forest floor to the towering treetops.

Many rainforest ant species are found nowhere else in the world. These include famous leafcutter ants, which use their jaws to chop up leaves and carry them back to their nest, the big-eyed *Gigantiops* and terrifying bullet ants, so named because their fierce sting feels like a GUNSHOT!

... rainforest?

Ants might be the most numerous rainforest insects, but MILLIONS of other species of insect call the rainforest home. In the Amazon rainforest alone, there are an estimated 370,000 different species of rainforest beetle, around 7,000 species of butterfly and 3,000 species of mosquito. BUZZ!

Can you get a coffee in the rainforest?

YES, THOUGH YOU MIGHT NEED TO BRING A CUP!
Coffee beans, which coffee comes from, grow well in the damp, shady conditions of the rainforest. And if you like to sprinkle a little cinnamon on your coffee, you can find that in the rainforest, too!

In fact, the rainforest gives us plenty of DELICIOUS food and drink. Fruits such as bananas, pineapples and avocados grow all over the rainforest, as do brazil nuts and açaí berries.

But the most famous food to come out of the rainforest is, of course, CHOCOLATE. The cacao plant grows in the wild across Central and South America. Its seeds are dried, roasted, shelled and ground before being made into chocolate bars. YUM!

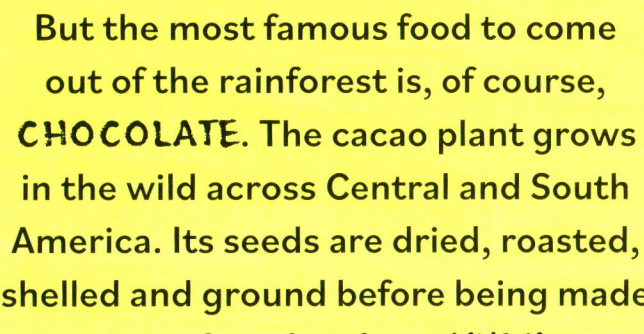

Spicy beans
Chocolate has been eaten in Central America since the time of the Maya 4,000 years ago. They made it into a hot frothy drink, spiced up with chilli.

Which sleepy animal only poos once a week?

THAT WOULD BE THE SLOTH! These slow, gentle mammals live high up in the rainforest trees, where they can sleep for 15 hours a day.

Sloths live on a diet of leaves, fruit and sap from nearby trees. It takes a long time for a sloth to digest food, so they only need to go to the toilet around **ONCE A WEEK**.

But a sloth's toilet trek is EPIC. Rather than relieve itself in the safety of the trees, a sloth very slowly makes its way down to the rainforest floor, where it risks being attacked by predators, such as eagles and jaguars. So why do they climb down from their safe perch? No one knows for sure, but sloths might use their wee and droppings to communicate with other sloths.

Take it slowww...
It can take a sloth a month to digest just one leaf!

Can you live in the rainforest?

YES, and some Indigenous peoples have done so for thousands of years. They range from the Yanomami peoples of the Amazon, to the Hongana Manyawa of Indonesia to the Baka peoples of Central and West Africa.

Some Indigenous peoples live a lifestyle like their ancestors would have done. They wear traditional clothes, hunt their food and live in simple homes, without electricity or running water. They live close to nature, using the RAINFOREST RESOURCES, such as plants and animals, carefully and sustainably.

Rainforest peoples' ways of life are at risk. Ranchers, and logging and mining companies have moved into the rainforest to cut down trees, create huge farms and build mines, taking away precious land from Indigenous peoples and changing the world they live in FOREVER.

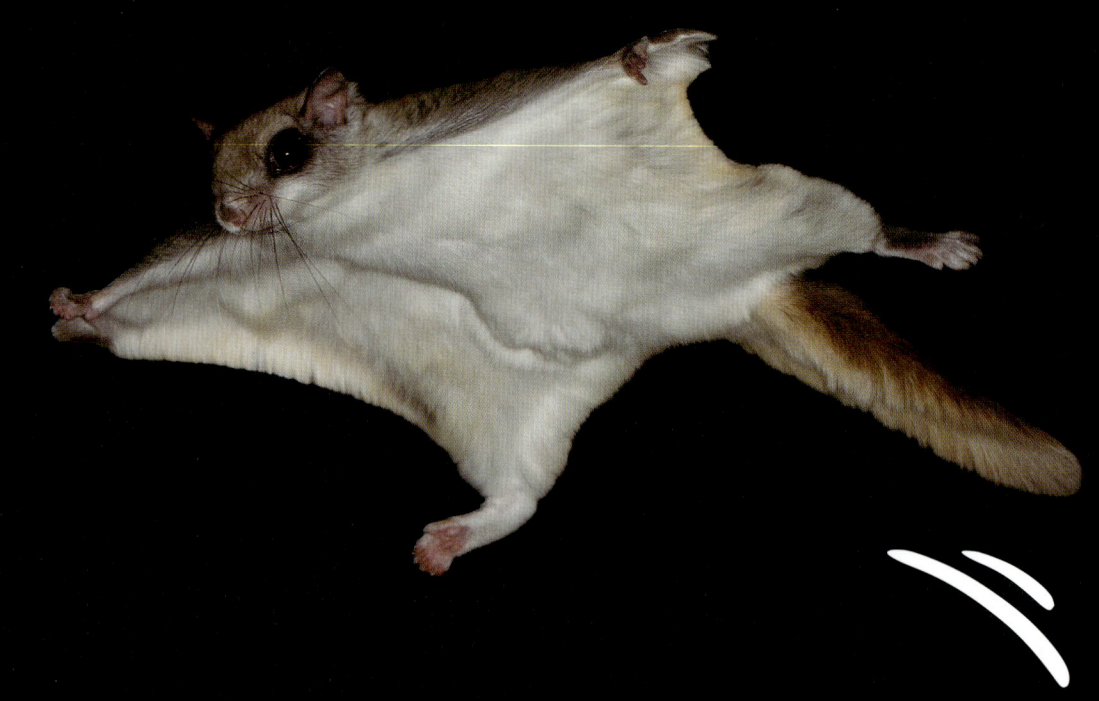

Which animal flies through the rainforest trees?

IT'S A BIRD ... IT'S A PLANE ... IT'S A ... SQUIRREL?

High up in the rainforest canopy, some species of squirrel (imaginatively called flying squirrels) appear to take to the air and fly from tree to tree. But can they really fly? The answer is: WELL YES, IN A WAY.

The difference between a flying squirrel and a bird or flying insect is that, unlike birds or insects, the squirrel doesn't have wings. Instead, it has a special furry layer of skin between its front and back legs. When it wants to go to another tree, the squirrel launches itself from a branch, stretching out its four legs and the connected skin to help it glide gently down to a tree or branch below. It steers itself using its legs, and its tail acts as a handy brake when it lands.
CLEVER SQUIRREL!

Gliders
Flying squirrels can glide through the air for up to 50 metres.

Where do apes sleep in nests?

When you think of nests, you probably think of birds. But a type of ape, called a BONOBO, makes its bed high in the rainforest canopy.

In the family
Bonobos and chimpanzees share 98.7 per cent of their DNA with humans.

Bonobos are only found in the rainforest surrounding the Congo River in Central Africa. These **ADORABLE** apes live in groups led by an older female bonobo.

During the day, bonobos share their favourite food of fruit on the rainforest floor. At night though, they climb high into the **RAINFOREST CANOPY** to build cosy nests made of branches and leaves. Sleeping together in the trees keeps the bonobos safe from predators on the ground, and helps them to look out for one another.

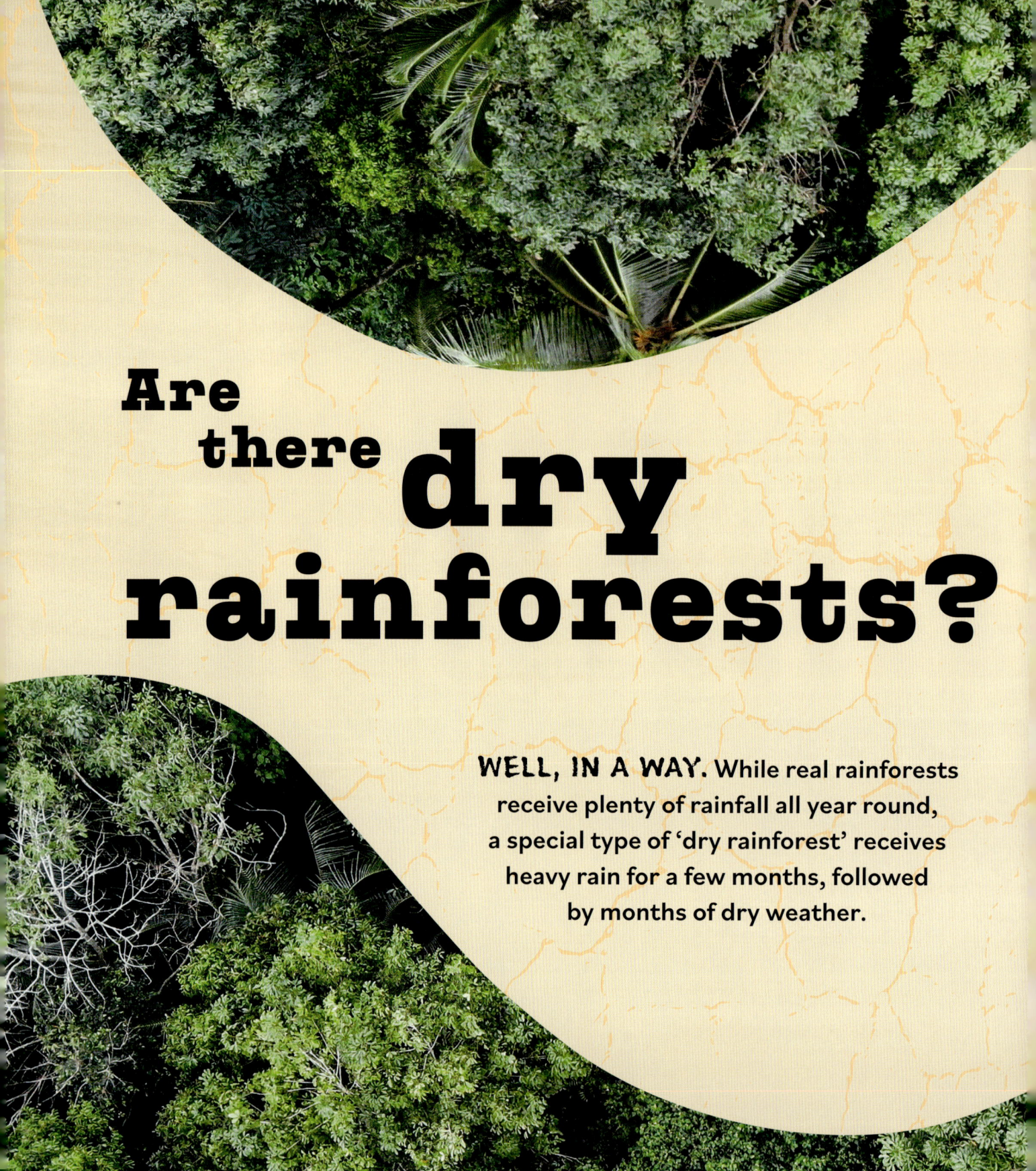

Are there dry rainforests?

WELL, IN A WAY. While real rainforests receive plenty of rainfall all year round, a special type of 'dry rainforest' receives heavy rain for a few months, followed by months of dry weather.

Dry rainforests aren't as rich in animal and plant life as other rainforests, but they are still home to thousands of species of insects, monkeys, deer, big cats and many different types of bird. Some have **CLEVERLY ADAPTED** to the forests' dry season. Frogs, for example, burrow deep into the mud and go to sleep (estivate) until the rains return.

These types of rainforest are found further from the equator than the tropical rainforest, where rainfall is more **SEASONAL**, in places like India, Mexico and north Australia. Trees here may shed their leaves to cope with the lack of rain, unlike the lush, leafy trees of the rainforest.

Just how poisonous is a poison dart frog?

VERY! These brightly-coloured amphibians may be tiny, but they are extremely toxic. The golden poison dart frog, for example, is just 5 CM long, but contains enough poison to kill ten adults!

Found in the rainforests of Central and South America, poison dart frogs spend their days in the leaf litter on the forest floor, hopping around after their prey of ants and other small insects. They don't use their poison, which is stored in their skin, to harm their prey. Instead, they whip out their **LONG, STICKY TONGUE** to capture it.

So why are these frogs **SO POISONOUS**? It keeps them safe! Their poison is fatal to all but one of their predators. Their bright colours warn predators to stay away!

Toxic spears
Some Indigenous rainforest peoples smear the frogs' poison on the tip of their spears before hunting.

How are rain- forests like lungs?

The huge, green rainforests don't seem to have a lot in common with our lungs. But in fact, they both help to keep humans, and EARTH ITSELF, alive.

Plants take in carbon dioxide gas and give out OXYGEN when they make food, during photosynthesis (see page 8). In humans it's the opposite, we breathe in oxygen into our lungs, and breathe out carbon dioxide.

Humans need to take in oxygen to make our bodies work and stay alive. So the fact that plants give out oxygen is INCREDIBLY useful to us. And rainforests contain half of all Earth's plant species, making them irreplaceable! We can't live without the rainforests, just like we can't live without our lungs.

Why are the rainforests disappearing?

The rainforests aren't vanishing overnight. It's not like a magic trick. But they are **SHRINKING FAST**. It's estimated that around 17 per cent of the Amazon rainforest has been lost in the last 50 years.

So why is this important habitat being destroyed? It's mainly due to farming. Huge cattle ranches are being built across the rainforest, with **SWATHES OF TREES** being cut down so the cows can graze. More rainforest is cleared to grow food for the cattle to eat.

The rainforest is also being cut down for its natural resources. Trees are felled for their wood, while mines are built to access **GOLD** and other minerals found below the rainforest soil.

Plenty is already being done to restrict farming, logging and mining in the rainforest. But more needs to happen. We can all help to **PROTECT THE RAINFORESTS** by eating less meat (in particular beef) and choosing rainforest-friendly products.

Glossary

Adaptation A change that helps a living thing to survive.

Algae A plant-like living thing that grows in water or damp places.

Amphibian Cold-blooded animals that can live on land and in water.

Canopy A thick layer of treetops.

Digest To break down food.

DNA A chemical found in the cells of living things.

Emergent layer The highest level of a forest, where the tallest trees grow.

Indigenous People who come from the place where they live, rather than moving to live there.

Leaf litter A layer of dead leaves and other plant matter found on the floor of a forest.

Mammal Warm-blooded animals with hair that feed their babies with their milk.

Minerals Materials that are found in the soil and in rocks.

Mining Digging into the ground to find useful or valuable materials.

Nutrients The goodness in food.

Oxygen A gas in air.

Parasite A plant or animal that lives on or in another and feeds off it.

Photosynthesis The process by which plants make food.

Poisonous Very harmful.

Pollinate To move pollen from one plant to another. Pollination is how plants reproduce (make new plants).

Predator An animal that hunts and eats other animals.

Prey An animal that is hunted and eaten by other animals.

Reptile Cold-blooded animals that are covered in scales and usually lay eggs.

Species Groups of living things that share similar features and are able to breed (have babies) together.

Traditional Beliefs and ways of life that have gone on for a long time without changing.

Vaccination Medicines, usually given by injection, which prevent us from getting some diseases.

Find out more!

WEBSITES

kids.nationalgeographic.com/nature/habitats/article/rain-forest
Rainforest information, videos, games and more.

rainforestfoundation.org/engage/kids/
Discover more about the rainforests and how we can all help to protect them.

www.youtube.com/watch?v=3vijLre760w
Watch the rainforest come to life in this video from National Geographic.

We strongly advise that Internet access is supervised by a responsible adult. The website addresses (URLs) included in this book were valid at the time of going to press. However, it is possible that contents or addresses may have changed since the publication of this book. No responsibility for any such changes can be accepted by either the author or the Publisher.

BOOKS

Explore Ecosystems: In a Rainforest by Sarah Ridley (Wayland, 2023)

Find the Funny: Life in the Rainforest by Anna Claybourne (Wayland, 2025)

The Rainforest Book by Charlotte Milner (DK Children, 2021)

Index

Africa 32, 37
Amazon rainforest 6-7, 27, 32, 45
  size 7, 45
Amazon River 7
amphibians 14, 16, 23, 39, 40-41
ants 26-27, 41
apes 36-37
  bonobos 36-37
  chimpanzees 37
Asia 5, 13, 39
Australia 5, 39

birds 11, 18, 22-23, 34-35, 39
Borneo rainforest 13
Brazil nuts 7, 28

carbon dioxide 42-43
Central America 18, 29, 37, 39, 41
chocolate 29
coffee 28
Congo rainforest 37
Congo River 37

dangers to rainforests 33, 45
deforestation 33, 45
diseases 20-21
DNA 37
dry rainforests 38-39

Earth 4, 6-7, 9, 26, 42-43
ecosystems 14
equator 4, 39

flowers 9, 12-13
flying squirrels 34-35
frogs 14, 16, 23, 39, 40-41
  poison dart 40-41

Goliath birdeater 22-23

Indigenous peoples 32-33, 41
insects 11, 13-14, 16, 20, 23, 26-27, 35, 39, 41

jaguars 11, 31
Jesus lizard 18-19

leaves 8, 11, 13-14, 16, 26, 30, 37, 39

mammals 11, 16, 23, 30-31, 34-37, 39
Maya 29
medicines 20-21
monkeys 11, 39

nutrients 13, 16-17

oxygen 42-43

photosynthesis 8, 42
plants 8-9, 11, 14, 16-17, 20-21, 28-29, 33, 39, 42-43
  bromeliads 14-15
  pitcher 16-17
poisonous animals 40-41
pollen/pollination 13
poo 17, 30-31

predators 18, 31, 37, 41
prey 16-17, 22, 41

Rafflesia flower 12-13
rain/rainwater 4-5, 9, 14, 38-39
rainforest layers 10-11, 25-26, 30-31, 34, 36, 41
reptiles 11, 18-19, 23
roots 8, 11, 13-14, 22, 25

seasons 9, 39
sloths 11, 30-31
soil 8, 16, 25, 45
South America 5, 7, 22, 29, 41

temperate rainforests 5
trees 6-7, 9, 11, 14, 20, 24-25, 30-31, 33-35, 37, 39, 45

venomous animals 22-23
vines 9, 11, 13, 24-25

water 8-9, 13, 14,-15, 8-19, 33
weather 4-5, 8-9, 38-39

48